A New True Book

THE HOPI

By Ann Heinrichs Tomchek

CHILDRENS PRESS ®

CHICAGO

A Hopi kachina carver

Dedicated to all who have known Koyaanisqatsi

PHOTO CREDITS

© Dugald Bremner—19

© Terry Eiler—23

© Reinhard Brucker—2

Marilyn Gartman Agency: © Michael P. Manheim—4 (bottom), 10, 26 (middle), 41 (left), 42 (left), 43 (right)

Historical Pictures Service, Chicago— 4 (top), 9

Museum of the American Indian—30 (2 photos), 31 (middle)

Odyssey Productions: © Robert Frerck—7, 33 (left); Edward S. Curtis Collection—12, 21 (top, bottom left, and bottom right), 26 (left)

Photo Source International: © Three Lions— Cover, 2

Photri: © Biedel—39 (top right and bottom left)

© H. Armstrong Roberts: 20, 24 (right)

© Charles Phelps Cushing—14, 35

© D. Muench—17

John Running: Photographer—24 (left), 31 (left and right), 33 (right), 36 (2 photos), 37 (left and top right), 39 (top left and bottom right), 41 (right), 42 (right), 43 (left), 45 (4 photos)

Tom Stack & Associates: © Suzi Barnes Moore—25 (right), 26 (right)

© Phil Welch—25 (left), 29, 37 (bottom right)

Cover: Hopi woman and child with baskets

Library of Congress Cataloging-in-Publication Data

Tomchek, Ann Heinrichs.
  The Hopi.

  (A New true book)
  Includes index.
  Summary: A brief history of the Hopi Indians describing their customs, religious beliefs, interactions with other tribes, and the changes modern civilization has brought to their traditional way of life.
    1. Hopi Indians—Juvenile literature. [1. Hopi Indians. 2. Indians of North America] I. Title.
E99.H7T66   1987   306'.08997   87-8037
ISBN 0-516-01234-7

Childrens Press®, Chicago
Copyright ©1987 by Regensteiner Publishing Enterprises, Inc.
All rights reserved. Published simultaneously in Canada.
Printed in the United States of America.
      15 16 17 18 19 20 R 02 01 00 99

TABLE OF CONTENTS

Dwellers of the High Mesas...5

The Peaceful People...8

Progressives and Traditionals...13

People of the Fourth World...16

Hopi Pueblos...20

The Kivas...22

Everyday Life...25

The Kachina Religion...29

The Calendar of Dances...32

Hopi Arts and Crafts...37

The Hopi Today...40

Words You Should Know...46

Index...48

Hopi village on Second Mesa (above)

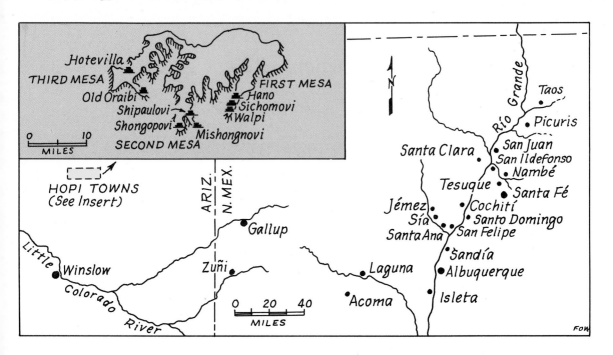

Hotevilla
THIRD MESA
FIRST MESA
Old Oraibi
Hano
Sichomovi
Shipaulovi
Walpi
Shongopovi
Mishongnovi
SECOND MESA
0   10
MILES

HOPI TOWNS
(See Insert)

ARIZ.
N. MEX.

Taos

Río Grande

Picuris

Santa Clara
San Juan
San Ildefonso
Nambé
Tesuque
Santa Fé
Jémez
Cochití
Sía
Santo Domingo
Santa Ana
San Felipe

Gallup

Sandía
Albuquerque

Little
Colorado
River

Winslow

Zuñi

Laguna

Isleta

0   20   40
MILES

Acoma

FOW

DWELLERS OF THE HIGH MESAS

In northeastern Arizona, at the southern end of Black Mesa, lies the land of the Hopi. There, rising sharply above the desert floor, are three steep, flat-topped mesas. The mesas are called simply First Mesa, Second Mesa, and Third Mesa.

Scattered across the three mesa tops are Hopi

villages, called pueblos. The pueblo of Oraibi, on Third Mesa, was started in the year 1050. It may be the oldest village in North America that has been lived in continuously. Other Hopi villages lie in the valleys beneath the mesas.

No one knows exactly where the Hopi came from. They belong to a group of Southwestern peoples called the Pueblo. But their language

Anasazi Ruins, Betatakin, Navajoland, Arizona

is different from other
Pueblo languages.

The Hopi's ancestors
were a people called the
Anasazi. Some ancient
Anasazi paintings tell the
same legends that are told
today in Hopi pueblos.

THE PEACEFUL PEOPLE

The name *Hopi* means good, peaceful, or wise. Throughout history, the Hopi have chosen to tend their crops rather than to make war.

In 1540, the Spanish explorer Francisco Vásquez de Coronado came to the Southwest. He was looking for the riches in the Seven Cities of Cibola.

Coronado and his soldiers searched the Southwest looking for the gold and other treasures said to be found in the Seven Cities of Cibola.

Coronado sent Pedro de Tovar into Hopi land to see if the riches were there. Disappointed, Tovar returned to Coronado.

Next, Coronado sent García López de Cárdenas to the Hopi. They led Cárdenas to the "great river"—the Grand Canyon.

The Grand Canyon seen from Hopi Point

Cárdenas was the first
white man to see the
canyon.

Other explorers followed.
The Hopi, fearing
punishment, often sent

them on with promises of
riches farther away. But
soon the Spanish claimed
the Hopi as their subjects.

In 1629, missionaries from
Spain arrived. They came to
convert the Hopi to Christianity.
The Hopi wanted to keep their
own religion, but they were
given little choice in the
matter.

In 1680 came the great
Pueblo Revolt. The Hopi,
along with the Utes and
the Navajo, killed three

missionaries and destroyed the missions.

Twelve years later, Spain sent Diego de Vargas to reconquer the Southwest. But the Hopi could not be reached. They had moved from the valleys to the high mesa tops. There they remained safe from Spanish attack.

Walpi, a Hopi settlement on First Mesa

PROGRESSIVES
AND TRADITIONALS

The 1700s were fairly peaceful for the Hopi. But trouble began again in the 1800s. Navajo, Apache, and Ute men raided Hopi villages. They killed many people and took others for trade as slaves.

Next, American explorers, soldiers, and government officials began to arrive. The late 1800s brought

Spectators watch the Hopi Snake Dance at the Walpi pueblo in 1897.

traders, tourists, teachers, and more missionaries.

The United States set up the Hopi reservation in 1882. Roads and schools were built. Many Hopi began to fear that their centuries-old way of life was in danger.

In 1906, in the village of

Oraibi, the Hopi held a contest. On one side were those who favored the new American influences. On the other side were the traditionals. The traditionals lost and founded, among others, the town of Hotevilla. This is still the most conservative of Hopi villages.

Today the Hopi remain divided. The progressives wish to work with outsiders. The traditionals hope to preserve ancient Hopi lands and customs.

PEOPLE OF THE FOURTH WORLD

According to Hopi legend, the first people were created in a dark cave far below the surface of the earth. They climbed up through two more caves along with the coyote, locust, spider, and other creatures until they reached the earth's surface. This is the Fourth World, the world we all live in today.

Moenkopi, a
Hopi village
in Arizona

The Hopi believe that
this Fourth World is
sacred. They believe that,
if their land is abused,
they will lose forever their
sacred way of life.

17

The Hopi say that when people came into the Fourth World, they climbed through a hole called the *sipapu*. But the *sipapu* is not just an imaginary hole. Deep in the Grand Canyon, near where the Colorado and the Little Colorado rivers meet, is a mound of earth. In the top of the mound is a hole about three feet across. The

The Hopi *sipapu* deep in the Grand Canyon

Hopi believe this is the original *sipapu*—the hole through which the human race was born. For the Hopi, it is the holiest spot on earth.

HOPI PUEBLOS

Hopi family photographed
outside their pueblo

East of the great *sipapu*, high atop the three mesas, stand the Hopi pueblos.

Some Hopi pueblos were built many centuries ago. Made of stones and mud, the pueblos may stand several stories high. Ladders lead from one story to the next.

Photographs taken by E. S. Curtis captured forever the Hopi pueblos at Mishongovi (above) and Walpi (below). The word *pueblo* is used to describe the village and the apartment-like buildings in the village.

THE KIVAS

Every Hopi pueblo has several underground chambers called kivas. Here the Hopi gather to talk and to take part in ancient religious ceremonies.

The Hopi have used kivas for hundreds of years. Ancient kivas have been found that are a thousand years old. Fabulous paintings of sacred animals

Although housed in the Museum of Northern Arizona in Flagstaff, this is actually a functioning kiva, where Hopi hold sacred ceremonies.

and spirits adorn the walls of some of these kivas.

One enters the kiva by climbing down a ladder. In the center of the kiva floor is a fire pit. At the south

Kiva wall painting (above) and an
1897 photograph of the sacred altar
in a kiva at the Walpi Pueblo

end is a bench for
spectators. At the north
end is a small hole in the
floor. This is a reminder of
the great *sipapu*, where
people first emerged from
below the earth.

EVERYDAY LIFE

Corn (maize) is the Hopi's basic food. It is so important that many Hopi religious ceremonies center around corn. The Hopi have twenty-four different kinds of corn. Blue and white corn are the most common.

Different kinds of corn are grown in the Hopi cornfield (left) at the foot of Second Mesa.

E. S. Curtis photographed a Hopi woman making *piki* (left). Today
Hopi women bake bread with yeast (middle) as well as *piki*.
A farmer (right) shows off his squash.

Women grind blue corn
into cornmeal to make thin,
paper-like *piki* bread.

Besides corn, the Hopi
raise beans, squash,
melons, gourds, pumpkins,
and fruits, such as
peaches and apricots,
brought by the Spanish.

Hopi men and women each have their special jobs. Women own the house and the land. They cook and weave baskets. Men plant and harvest crops, weave cloth, and perform most of the religious ceremonies.

Many Hopi also raise sheep and cattle.

When a Hopi baby is born, it is given a special blanket and a perfect ear of corn. Early in the morning of its 20th day, the baby is taken to the mesa cliff and held up to face the rising sun. As the first rays strike its forehead, the baby is given its names.

Hopi children attend school, but they also learn the ancient Hopi ways. Boys learn Hopi religious rituals and men's crafts in the kivas. Girls learn to grind corn, bake, and weave in the home.

Ancient rock carvings of kachinas on Third Mesa

THE KACHINA RELIGION

At the heart of Hopi religious life are the kachinas. Kachinas are powerful ancestor spirits. They may be called upon to bring rain, drive out sickness, or make crops grow.

Mixed Kachina Dance painted by Ray Naha (above) and the Hano Clown Kachina (right) are in the collection of the National Museum of the American Indian in New York City.

For religious ceremonies, kachina dancers paint their bodies and wear masks. Feathers, jewelry, and woven fabrics are used to create special kachinas. There are over three hundred different kachinas. Some of them are the

Stone-Eater, the Ogre Woman, the Mud Head, the Wolf, and the Buffalo.

The Hopi make kachina dolls, too. Some are given to young Hopi girls during kachina ceremonies. Others are sold to tourists.

Kachina dolls: Antelope (left), Mud Head (middle), and Crow Mother (right)

THE CALENDAR OF DANCES

The Hopi call upon their spirits through dances. Many Hopi celebrate New Year on Soyal, around December 21. The Hopi believe the kachinas come out from the underworld at this time.

January brings the Buffalo Dance and the Social Dance.

Buffalo dancers

February is the month of the
Bean Dance, or Powamu.
During Powamu, children of
six or seven are brought
into the kachina religion.
First, the kachinas scare the

children. Then they give them kachina dolls and toys. On the last night, the dancers take off their masks. Then the children learn that kachinas are villagers dressed up as spirits.

March through early summer is the time for the Plaza Dances. Long lines of kachinas dance through the village plaza, praying for rain and good crops.

In July the Hopi have the home-going ceremony.

1896 photograph of the Hopi Snake Dance

The first corn has ripened
and the kachinas return
to their spirit world.

August brings the Snake
Dance. Calling for rain,
dancers hold live snakes in
their mouths. In September
and October, the Hopi have
the women's dances—

35

Hopi
Butterfly
dancers

the Basket Dance and
the Butterfly Dance.

In November comes
Wuwuchim. At this time,
after long hard tests of
strength, young men officially
become adults. Wuwuchim
is a sign that the Hopi way
of life will survive.

HOPI ARTS AND CRAFTS

The Hopi arts show a
rich love of beauty. Their
silver jewelry has designs
of spiritual creatures,
birds, and other animals.

Hopi artists create beautiful objects in silver.

Hopi men weave robes, sashes, kilts, and leggings to use in religious ceremonies. Each pattern and color has a spiritual meaning.

Hopi women weave baskets with yucca leaves and various grasses.

Hopi potters follow designs that were used hundreds of years ago. Using sweeping curves, they picture birds, flowers, human forms, and ceremonial scenes.

Hopi craftsmen use traditional designs on their
pottery and include them in the objects they weave.

Many Hopi artists today
use designs like those
painted on Anasazi kiva
walls a thousand years ago.

THE HOPI TODAY

The Hopi today are a proud people. They love their traditions, their arts, and their land. But they are also very much a part of modern American life.

Hopi children attend schools on the reservation or in nearby towns. Modern medical centers take care of health needs.

Many Hopi live and work outside the reservation.

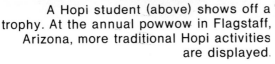
A Hopi student (above) shows off a trophy. At the annual powwow in Flagstaff, Arizona, more traditional Hopi activities are displayed.

They come back for special religious celebrations. Other Hopi work on the reservation—in government offices, at the Hopi Cultural Center, or in their homes.

Today Rita Nuvangyaoma weaves and Kenny Lucas
carves kachinas at the Hopi Cultural Center.

At the Hopi Cultural
Center, on Second Mesa,
tourists can watch Hopi
artists at work and
learn about Hopi culture.
But many problems
remain. Outside companies

Hopi construction workers
build modern structures
on Second Mesa.

explore Hopi land for the
valuable minerals there.
Many Hopi, believing that
their land is sacred,
oppose this.

Troubles with the Navajo,
whose reservation
surrounds the Hopi's,
continue today, as well.

For a century, the two groups have argued about their boundaries. Today the U.S. government is trying to draw the borders more fairly. Bitter feelings arise as people are moved to other locations.

Still, the Hopi look to the future with hope. The "peaceful people" are also a proud people—proud to have kept their ancient

customs alive and proud
to be the Hopi—yesterday,
today, and always.

WORDS YOU SHOULD KNOW

ancestors(AN • sess • terz) — all persons in a family who live or have lived before one's own birth

ancient(AIN • shent) — very old

basic(BAY • sik) — main, of first importance

bitter(BIT • er) — unpleasant, hard to take, harsh

boundaries(BOUN • dreez) — the outer limits of an area; its borders on all sides

canyon(KAN • yun) — very deep, narrow area surrounded by high cliffs

centuries(SEN • shreez) — periods of one hundred years

common(KAH • mun) — most usual, same, seen most often

conservative(kun • SIR • vi • tiv) — traditional, those who would not accept or welcome changes

continuously(kun • TIN • yoo • us • lee) — lasting a long time, happening without stop

convert(kun • VERT) — to change completely, to turn to another form, as a religion

crafts(KRAFTS) — handmade items made by special skills in art and workmanship

customs(KUSS • tumz) — practices carried on for a long time

emerged(ih • MERJD) — came out of, arose, came into view

explorer(ex • PLOR • er) — one who searches, travels in an unknown territory

fabric(FAB • rik) — the cloth used in making garments

grind(GRYND) — to pound or crush

harvest(HAR • vist) — gather in, as crops, when fully ripened

history(HISS • tree) — a branch of learning that deals with the past events of a people, a territory, or any particular subject

influence(IN • floo • ense) — put pressure on to accept changes by using power, example, or inspiration

language(LANG • gwidj) — the spoken or written method of communicating among people of the same community or cultural background

legends(LEH • jenz) — popular stories handed down through generations, whether true or fanciful

mesa(MAY • sa) — Spanish word meaning "table." Seen most often in Southwest states — high, flat land formation with sharp, steep sides, appearing like a table

mound(MOUND) — a small hill

oppose(uh • POHZE) — to be or act against

plazas(PLA • zahz) — open space or squares, usually in the center of a town

preserve(prih • ZERV) — to keep, to hold on to

progressives(pruh • GRESS • ivz) — those persons favoring making changes to better their conditions

proud(PROUD) — feeling satisfied for having accomplished something; having high regard for one's importance; self-respect

pueblo(PWEB • lo) — Spanish word meaning town or people

reservation(reh • zer • VAY • shun) — an area for use of Native Americans

ritual(RIT • choo • el) — usual way of performing a ceremony; manner in which an act is practiced

sacred(SAY • krid) — holy, revered

subjects(SUB • jekts) — persons who have been overpowered and are ruled by others

survive(sir • VYVE) — to continue to live after some serious problem or event

terrorize(TAIR • er • rize) — frighten, to cause fear

traditional(truh • DISH • un • il) — handed down for a long time

valleys(VAL • eez) — the low points between mountain ranges, often with a stream or river running at their bottom

INDEX

Americans, 13, 15
Anasazi, 7, 39
animals, paintings of, 22-23
Apache, 13
Arizona, 5
arts, artists, 37-39, 40, 42
babies, 27-28
baking, 28
Basket Dance, 36
Bean Dance, 33
Black Mesa, 5
boundaries, Hopi-Navajo, 44
boys, 28
bread, 26
Buffalo, kachina, 31-33
Butterfly Dance, 36
Canyon, Grand, 9-10, 18
de Cárdenas, García, 9-10
cattle raising, 27
ceremonies, 22, 25, 27, 28, 30-32, 34-35, 38, 41
children, 27-28, 33-34, 40
Christianity, 11
Cibola, Seven Cities of, 8
cloth, weaving of, 27
Colorado rivers, 18
corn, 25-27, 28, 35

de Coronado, Francisco, 8-9
crafts, 37-39
creation, belief in, 16-19
crops, 8, 27, 29, 35
customs, 44-45
dances, 32-36
dolls, kachina, 31, 34
everyday life, 25-28
explorers, American, 13
fire pit, 23
First Mesa, 5
food, 25-27
Fourth World, 16-19
fruit, 26
girls, 28, 31
Grand Canyon, 9-10, 18
"great river," 9
health, 40
home-going ceremony, 34
Hopi
  ancestors, 7
  Cultural Center, 41-42
  land of the, 5, 15, 17
  meaning of name, 8
  origin, 6
  reservation, 14
  subjects of Spain, 11
Hotevilla, 15
human race, beginning of, 19
Indian, Pueblo, 6

jewelry, 30, 37
jobs, 26-27, 40-41
kachinas, 29-36
kivas, 22-24, 28, 39
land, 5, 15, 17, 40, 43
language, 7
legends, 7, 16
life, daily, 25-28, 40
Little Colorado, 18
masks, 34
men, 26-27, 28, 36, 38
mesa, 5, 20, 28, 42
minerals, 43
missionaries, 11, 14
naming of baby, 28
Navajo, 11, 13, 43
New Year, 32
Oraibi pueblo, 6, 15
"peaceful people", 8-12, 44
piki bread, 26
Plaza Dances, 34
potters, 38
Powamu, dance, 33
progressives, 15
Pueblo
  paintings, ancient, 7, 22-23
  Indians, 6-7
  Revolt, 11
pueblos, 6, 20, 22
rain, praying for, 29, 34-35
religious beliefs, 22, 25-28, 29-31, 32-36

reservation, 14, 40-41
Revolt, Pueblo, 11
schools, 28, 40
Second Mesa, 42
sheep raising, 27
sickness, 29, 40
silver, 37
sipapu, 18-20, 24
slaves, 13
Snake Dance, 35
Social Dance, 32
Southwest, 12
Soyal, 32
Spain, 8-12
spirits, ancestor, 29, 34, 35
  paintings of, 23
summer, 34
sun, 28
teachers, 14
tourists, 14, 42
de Tovar, Pedro, 9
toys, 34
traders, 14
traditionals, 15, 40
Utes, 11, 13
de Vargas, Diego, 12
villages, Hopi, 5-6, 15, 34
war, 8
weaving, 28, 38
women, 26, 35, 38
work, 26-27, 40-41
Wuwuchim, 36

About the Author

Ann Heinrichs Tomchek grew up in Arkansas. She received a Bachelor of Music degree from St. Mary's College in Notre Dame, Indiana, and a Master of Music degree in Piano Performance from the American Conservatory of Music in Chicago. Ms. Tomchek has been a composer, piano recitalist, and music critic, and her reviews and feature articles have appeared in many newspapers and magazines. She is presently a free-lance editor and writer, living in Illinois.